I AM UNDETERRED

I AM UNDETERRED

My Success Plan

RANIA HABIBY ANDERSON

Author of **Undeterred**

The Way Women Work Press

The Way Women Work Press books are available at special discounts when purchased in bulk for premiums and sales promotions as well as for fund-raising or educational use. Special editions or book excerpts can also be created to specification. For details, contact orders@thewaywomenwork.com.

The Way Women Work Press
www.thewaywomenwork.com
www.undeterredwomen.com

Cover design: Carter Schwarberg
Interior design: Andrew Pautler, Pautler Design
Author photo: Jenny Wheat

978-0-9909063-3-9 (paperback)
978-0-9909063-4-6 (ebook)

Library of Congress Control Number: 2014957523

CONTENTS

HABIT 3 Focus

HABIT 4 Integrate

HABIT 5 Accelerate

HABIT 6   Lead

MESSAGE TO THE READER

WOMEN IN EMERGING ECONOMIES HAVE UNPRECEDENTED opportunities available to them today. With new markets opening up around the world and businesses expanding their infrastructures, the demand for skilled, well-educated professionals has far outpaced the supply. Thus, women in developing nations who wish to advance in corporate careers or to own and operate their own businesses have more options than ever before. As traditional female roles are giving way to new roles, women sometimes confront obstacles and resistance. Those who succeed persevere by inventing solutions and workarounds that make sense within the contexts of their own cultures.

Compiled from the results of in-depth study and interviews conducted over a span of four years with more than 250 professional women at different stages in their lives and careers, I identified six habits shared by successful women, which are described in my book *Undeterred*. This workbook contains all of the same exercises as you will find in *Undeterred*. They have been pulled out and compiled here in the format of a workbook with lots of blank space for you to write your reflections, capture information, and make lists of the actions you plan to take.

I am delighted that you have chosen to gather your thoughts and develop your success plan using this workbook. As I compiled the exercises, I envisioned and hoped that you would use this notebook in the same way you might use a journal. Write down whatever comes to mind, whenever it does. Write or draw in the margins, highlight, and add in mentions of articles, quotes, or comments about the exercises that inspire and guide you.

When you develop and *implement* your personal Undeterred Action Plan, you will create positive change for yourself. Remember that it will take consistently implementing all six of the success habits to achieve the success you envision for yourself as you are planning.

66

Adopt your own success habits

The six success habits that you will be practicing as you work through the exercises are:

Habit 1: Be Undeterred. Being undeterred means persevering despite impediments and setbacks, and being resolute about what you want. Undeterred women don't just go to work and try to survive the experience; they learn how to prosper and excel in their roles. They're not resigned to the problems that confront them; they thrive in spite of them. Whereas many women in the same circumstances fail to fulfill their professional promise, undeterred women flourish.

Habit 2: Prepare. Undeterred women work extremely hard to be as prepared as possible by developing the knowledge, skills, drive, and contacts they need to succeed. They prepare themselves for the difficult circumstances and obstacles they know they will encounter, as well as for the opportunities they will create or find. They recognize that for them, and women like them, the path to success cannot be left to chance. Opportunity + preparation = achievement.

Habit 3: Focus. Undeterred women define success on their own terms and in ways they find personally meaningful. They set clear goals and establish plans to achieve what they want. They understand why and how they want to pursue their goals. They regularly evaluate the value of the rewards associated with their success and strive to find contentment in their lives.

Habit 4: Integrate. Undeterred women believe work-life integration is attainable. They know, and prove by example every day, that it is possible to have successful careers despite also having other life priorities. Furthermore, they take good advantage of the changes in the modern workplace to create their integrated lives. They are not governed by the past, by tradition, or by ideas of what women should or should not do and can or cannot do. They design their lifestyles to blend their office time with their personal lives, their time at home with their work.

Habit 5: Accelerate. Acceleration is the most tangible and straightforward of the success habits. Undeterred women strategically implement a set of specific and well-defined, time-tested actions, including delivering tangible results, making their accomplishments known, asking for what they want, taking on high-profile assignments, and building strong support networks.

Habit 6: Lead. Undeterred women view themselves as having the ability to be role models and make a contribution or a difference. They lead from the position they are in, regardless of what it is. They start by envisioning a better future and create new paths for themselves and others. Then they take the initiative to generate ideas, be resourceful, and innovate or make improvements to create the results they envision.

From Abuja to Amman, from Bangalore to Beijing, from Beirut to Buenos Aires, from Cairo to Croatia, from Johannesburg to Jakarta, from Moscow to Mumbai, from Nairobi to New Delhi, from Saint Petersburg to Sofia, and from Shanghai to Sao Paulo, women who are architects, attorneys, corporate executives, journalists, scientists, doctors, small business owners, and technologists, ranging in age from twenty-five to sixty-five, are using these habits to be successful on their own terms. These are women from neighborhoods and families like your own, who work at all levels of corporations, run businesses, and work independently as consultants and freelancers.

Now it's your turn. In *I Am Undeterred*, you'll find self-reflection exercises paired with a list of action steps—all designed to help you develop a success plan for building an enriching and professionally satisfying life that you love. Work on developing your success plan on your own or with a group of likeminded friends or colleagues, and discuss your success plan with your mentor or coach. Also remember, your sustained success in the future is just a matter of consistently executing these same few key success habits and staying the course until you attain your ultimate goals.

Use this workbook to establish a strong foundation of self. If you don't believe in yourself, no one else will believe in you. Unless you first give yourself a chance, no one else will give you a chance. If you question your abilities, so will everyone else. As you gain self-confidence you will move forward more easily through any challenges that come up in your career. As you move forward, new and exciting opportunities will open up for you.

One of the things that women (and men) around the world often say when they are asked about their success is, "I was lucky." *Luck* has been defined as what happens when preparation meets opportunity. But as South African Tebogo Mashego said during my interview with her, "Success is not about luck. It's about working hard, persistence, actions, beliefs, and habits."

This journal is designed to help you develop your own beliefs, actions, and habits. You are in a time and place where success is possible for you, so be undeterred in pursuit of your success!

Rania

— HABIT 1: BE UNDETERRED —

Clear the Obstacles

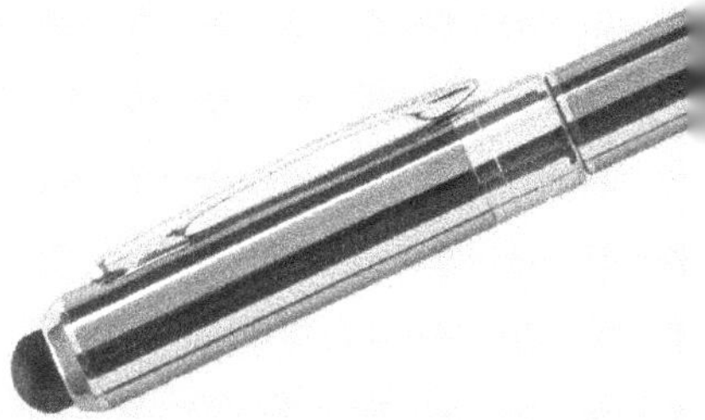

AN UNDETERRED MINDSET IS THE KEYSTONE OF SUCCESS. To succeed, you don't have to eliminate all the obstacles or get everything right. Try changing your perspective about the obstacles and take actions that move you forward, around, or through them. Regularly looking for solutions has the power to transform everything for you.

Millions of women are figuring out how to get through and around obstacles. There is no doubt that you can, too! If you have been letting obstacles block your path it is now time to build an undeterred mindset by taking the repeated actions to establish the habits for your success.

The thoughts you think and the actions you take on a regular basis influence your brain. Over time, new responses and routines will override old patterns that formerly got in your way. Believing you can clear obstacles will change your responses to them and prevent them from stopping you.

The two most important questions to ask yourself are:

- Which of my typical responses to challenges and obstacles do I want to change?
- What specific actions or responses will I start taking from here forward to clear the obstacles I encounter?

It is time for you to develop ways to clear obstacles. Here's how.

SELF-REFLECTION:
HOW CAN YOU BE UNDETERRED?

The two parts of being undeterred are:

- An undeterred mindset.
- Clearing obstacles.

Developing an undeterred mindset is about how you see obstacles and what you think about them. To assess your perception of the obstacles you face, ask yourself the following questions.

- What is my immediate professional or business goal?
  Examples: Get a job, a promotion, a raise, or a business license. Start or grow a business. Make more money.

- What main obstacle is presently in my way?
  Examples: A person, a regulation, a particular bias, a financial need, or a lack of knowledge or confidence.

- When faced with this type of obstacle, how do I usually react?
  Examples: Anger, frustration, immobilization, blame, giving up, or confrontation.

- On the rare occasions when I encounter this challenge, how do I work differently?
  Examples: I come up with alternatives. I work more creatively. I work with someone else.

- When I see others who overcome this challenge, what do I see them doing?
  Examples: They seek out alternatives. They are not bothered by the challenge. They find a way to turn the obstacle into an opportunity for themselves. They seek advice from knowledgeable people.

With your answers to the preceding questions in mind, decide what actions would best help you. Following are some ideas.

ACTIONS
TO CLEAR OBSTACLES

Train yourself to keep going when you encounter obstacles. If you don't stop, you will find or create solutions to reach your objectives. The key questions to ask yourself are:

- What one thing could I do to go around, overcome, or remove the obstacle I've identified?
- What can I change?

As you answer these questions, you'll discover that there are five primary ways to overcome obstacles.

Remove the obstacle. Based on what you know or from talking with others, is there a way you can eliminate the obstacle or convince someone else to change the system, policy, or procedure that's in your way?

Find a workaround. What process or alternative way could you use to go around the obstacle?

Negotiate an exception. Ask if it would be possible for you not to go by the rule or requirement that's getting in your way. Be sure to provide a reason for asking for this exception and the benefit of you taking the course of action.

Leave. Is there somewhere else you could work to avoid or minimize this obstacle?

Do the opposite. It has been said, "Insanity is doing the same thing over and over again and expecting different results."

If something is not working, we cannot expect a different outcome from doing what we usually do. We have to do something different. The undeterred mindset is often best developed by using a technique I call *Do the Opposite*, in which you decide to try a different approach purposefully to see if you get a better result. In the table below are some specific "opposite" actions to get you started.

IF YOU USUALLY . . .	DO THE OPPOSITE:
Assume it isn't possible to overcome the obstacle	Envision yourself achieving what you want. *Ask yourself or someone you trust if there is a way to make the obstacle you're facing easier to deal with, even if it cannot be removed.*
Keep quiet about the obstacle	Talk about it with someone who can address it. *Depending on your situation, it may be most appropriate to talk with the person who has created the challenge or with your manager, a member of the human resources staff in your company, a government official, or an organization focused on the issue.*
Incessantly talk about the obstacle, expressing a great deal of frustration	Express your frustration through silence. *This approach may be particularly helpful during meetings or in a corporate setting, as your silence will likely feel uncomfortable to the person demonstrating the bias.*
Don't know enough about an issue or obstacle you are encountering	Learn more about it. *Research to learn where it comes from, how it started, and what those who created the obstacle are afraid of or guarding against.*
Stop when you encounter a particular obstacle	Go one additional step beyond where you would normally go. *If you typically only try once, then try twice. If you typically stop when you are told no, ask one more time.*

Avoid confrontation	Address the issue head on. *If you typically accept biases in your workplace, for instance, express your frustration verbally or in writing.*
Defer to the judgments of others	Clearly express your opinion. *Say, "Here's how I view the situation" or "Here's another way to think about this issue." Or ask, "Have you thought about the issue from this perspective?"*
Blame others or the system	Examine what you yourself could do differently. *Look at your own behavior and figure out one thing you can do differently to achieve your goals.*
Continually think about the problems you encounter	Think about a possible solution. *Reflect on ways you could minimize the challenge, or do your best to come up with an alternative.*

66

Develop an undeterred mindset

Prepare

Preparation builds confidence,
courage, and competence.

ONE OF THE FIRST THINGS WOMEN IN GROWTH economies usually share with me is that lack of preparation has never been an option for them. A woman who wants a career or business in a growth economy simply won't succeed if she is *unprepared*.

Data from the International Labor Organization, a United Nations agency that tracks the global workforce, reveals two main reasons some women don't pursue work. They either are not prepared or don't have the resources or infrastructure they need to join the workforce.[1] Women thriving in their workplaces and succeeding in business have overcome these obstacles through consistent implementation of a powerful set of habits.

Confidence:
Believe in Yourself

Y OU HAVE THE ABILITY TO DEVELOP YOUR SELF-CONFIDENCE. By reprogramming your brain to reduce negative thoughts and emotions, and taking the risk to move toward your goals every day, you will begin to trust this capacity. You will then be able to pursue your goals even if you still have some self-doubt. Each of your accomplishments, no matter how small it is, will build the confidence you need to tackle larger and more difficult challenges.

Confidence is built step by step through thought, word, and deed. Practice thinking with confidence by quieting your self-judging inner voice. Practice speaking with confidence by using self-affirming phrases with a strong, open posture. Act with confidence by learning new skills and trying new things. The more you think, speak, and act with confidence, the more confident you will feel.

To prepare for success, build your confidence and address your fears. Without confidence and courage it's easy to become paralyzed and get stuck in a place that you don't believe you can get out of. Undeterred women who have developed confidence and courage keep moving forward even in the face of self-doubt. Once you have a balanced and realistic sense of self-confidence, take the other preparatory actions that will build the foundation for your success. Here's how.

SELF-REFLECTION:
ARE YOU UNDERMINING YOUR CONFIDENCE?

Start by examining your thoughts and behavior. Ask:

- Do I trust myself, or am I constantly second-guessing every move I want to make?

- Do I consciously or subconsciously underestimate my abilities?

- Do I blame myself for mistakes?

- Do I negatively judge myself and regularly engage in negative self-talk?

- What does the voice inside my head say?
  - Is it critical or supportive?
  - How strong is it?
  - How much do I listen to it?

- Who or what helps me turn down or silence its negative messages?

- Do I think that people are or are not naturally confident? And have I decided that I don't have enough self-confidence to do what I want to do?

- Do I blame others, my society, culture, parents, and/or men, for my lack of achievement?

If you answered yes to any of these questions, it is an indication that you are undermining your confidence to some degree.

ACTIONS
THAT BUILD CONFIDENCE

To build your self-assurance, start thinking, speaking, and acting with confidence. Pick and commit to consistently taking the actions that most resonate and apply to you from the following list of ideas, tips, and techniques.

Think with confidence. Identify your strengths, then remember them as you talk with others.

- Ask: What are my strengths?
  Examples: working with people, quantitative analysis, coming up with ideas, implementing ideas, managing projects, writing, technology, science, sales.

- Ask: What are my best characteristics or qualities?
  Examples: I am very smart, kind, hardworking, exciting, thoughtful, positive, charismatic, creative, and so on.

- Control your thoughts about yourself. With practice, you can learn to direct the way you think about yourself.

  ▪ Use positive, kind, and encouraging words when you talk to yourself.

  ▪ Don't dwell on mistakes you have made in the past. Instead, identify what you would do differently in the future.

  ▪ Repeat positive statements or affirmations about yourself. Start those statements with the phrases like "I can," "I am," or "I will."
  Examples: "I can get a new job," "I will get a promotion." "I can secure funding for my business." "I can accomplish this goal." "I am prepared for success." "I can see the path forward." "I am grateful for who I am and what I can accomplish." "I can change X." "I can overcome this obstacle."

  ▪ Mentally prepare. Come up with and rehearse the specific steps you need to take to accomplish a task.

- Envision yourself succeeding at a task or accomplishing a goal you have set.

- Know that it is inevitable that you will not succeed at everything and that some things will go wrong. Tell yourself that mistakes and failure are normal, that you will learn from the hardships you encounter and that you are capable of finding new solutions.

66

Prepare for your success with confidence and competence.

- Think positively—remember that undeterred women are resilient in the face of obstacles and are able to find solutions.

Speak with confidence. Even when you don't feel completely confident, it's important to talk about your strengths, qualities, and what you can do, rather than about what you cannot do. Use phrases like: *"I can," "I am able to," "I am confident that I can," "I feel strongly that," "I know that."* These are called affirmations.

- Share how you will do a task, rather than revealing your doubts.

- Stand or a sit in the way that makes you feel confident when you are speaking.

- Don't add a question at the end of a statement or apologize when sharing your perspective.
- Say your affirmations out loud to yourself.

Act with confidence. Implement a regular confidence-building routine. These routines are proven to work for people. Select and implement ones that you believe will be most helpful to you.

- Read motivational quotes.

- Read books that give you ideas, hope, and inspiration.

- Exercise.

- Dress in a way that makes you feel more confident.

- Write down your affirmations and put them in places at home and work where you can see them.

- Establish a meditation practice during which you focus on your affirmations, confidence, and goals, and on your gratitude for what you are capable of and have already achieved.

- Build your knowledge and skills.

- Practice what you plan to say or do. Sometimes I practice in front a of mirror so I can see myself saying the words, and can work on my tone of voice and my body language.

- Observe people you deem confident. How do they behave? Adopt or adapt similar behaviors that boost your level of confidence.

- Make an appointment with someone confident whom you admire. Ask her (or him) how she builds her self-confidence.

- Challenge yourself to do things professionally that you are not comfortable doing.

- Try. Even if you are not sure you can succeed, even if you have self-doubt or reservation. As long as you have prepared, move forward.

- Accept responsibility for failures and learn from your mistakes, but don't blame yourself or doubt your ability to succeed in the future.

- Stretch yourself by taking an additional step beyond what you normally take after achieving success with something you are good at. Ask: What else would I do if I felt confident?

Prepare

Preparation builds confidence,
courage, and competence.

ONE OF THE FIRST THINGS WOMEN IN GROWTH economies usually share with me is that lack of preparation has never been an option for them. A woman who wants a career or business in a growth economy simply won't succeed if she is *unprepared*.

Data from the International Labor Organization, a United Nations agency that tracks the global workforce, reveals two main reasons some women don't pursue work. They either are not prepared or don't have the resources or infrastructure they need to join the workforce.[1] Women thriving in their workplaces and succeeding in business have overcome these obstacles through consistent implementation of a powerful set of habits.

Courage: Move Through Fear

THERE ARE THREE VERY IMPORTANT STRATEGIES TO PREPARE FOR success: moving forward in spite of your fears, identifying your motivations, and having a strong support system. The following exercises are designed to help you take your courage to a new level.

The remedy for fear is action. You will succeed if you face what you are afraid of and continue to move toward your goals no matter what type of challenges you encounter. To take action when you feel afraid, simply push yourself to go one step beyond the point where your instincts tell you to stop. Then take one more step beyond that. And then . . . you guessed it . . . one more after that. As you do so, you'll see that you are capable of moving forward in spite of fear.

Fear and doubt cannot be entirely eradicated; they will always continue to exist alongside our actions as we move toward our goals. The good news is that when we pursue our purpose, we stop fueling our fears and doubts. Fear is not actually something to overcome; it is an emotion to work through.

Remember, no one can motivate you as much as you can motivate yourself. If you want to succeed, be resilient and undeterred. You can also gain courage from other people. It is therefore important to surround yourself with people who appreciate and respect your aspirations, and to keep your distance from those who don't.

SELF-REFLECTION: HOW CAN YOU BRING YOUR FEARS INTO THE OPEN?

If you can accurately identify your fears and pinpoint why they exist, you can address them and make more rational business decisions. It doesn't matter whether you fear rejection, failure, or something else. Bringing your fear out into the open is the first step. Knowing is better than not knowing.

Here are some questions to ask.

- What do I fear the most?
  Examples: failure, financial instability, or not being able to find another job.

- What am I worried about?
  Examples: what people will say about me, my reputation, that failure is not understood or acceptable in my country.

- What is the worst that could happen if I proceed with my goal?
  Examples: I could lose my job or run out of money.

- Why am I afraid I can't succeed?
  Example: I don't think I have all the information, skills, or contacts I need.

- What am I afraid will happen if I become really successful?
  Example: People will think I care more about my career than my family.

- Why am I afraid that I won't be able to manage at home if I am successful?
  Examples: I don't have a supportive husband or family.

ACTIONS
TO BUILD COURAGE

After you have answered the preceding self-reflection questions, then:

- Identify what makes you feel strong.
  Examples: having knowledge and information, building time into my schedule to research and gather information.

- Build rituals, practices, or processes that help you work through your fears.
  Examples: doing research, talking with people I trust, praying, or meditating.

SELF-REFLECTION: WHAT MOTIVATES YOU?

You will build your ability to take courageous action only when you know why you want what you want. Think about what motivates you. Ask: "What motivates me?" Is it any of the following things?

- A sense of achievement
- Recognition
- Money
- Power
- Influence
- Having independence
- Learning and mastering new things
- Setting an example
- Having a sense of purpose or making a difference
- Wanting to leave a legacy

ACTIONS TO STAY MOTIVATED

Any time you encounter an obstacle or a personal detractor, any time you are afraid, think about the reasons behind your work. When you focus on why something is so important to you, you will be more able to find solutions to get what you want. You will also have the courage to take action in spite of the difficulties or your fears.

SELF-REFLECTION:
DO YOU NEED MORE SUPPORT?

Supportive people around you will encourage you, and enable you, to take courageous action. To create a support system, ask:

- Are the people around me supportive of my professional aspirations?

- Am I spending time with people who have similar goals as I have, both in type and in size?

If the answer to either of these questions is no, take some or all of the following actions.

ACTIONS
TO BUILD YOUR SUPPORT

Here are some ways to build the support you need.

- Seek out friends and extended family members, both male and female, who are working, perhaps including professors from your university. Speak with them about your professional aspirations.

66

Don't let others stop or discourage you from pursuing what you want.

- Join business organizations that provide services for women and social networks that support women's careers and/or businesses online and in person.

- Reach out to connect with working women in your country and region. These could be peers or women who have already established themselves professionally.

- Connect and build a relationship with someone who can be a mentor to you.

- Read about the professional paths of other working women. You can find lots of examples online, including at TheWayWomenWork.com.

- Ignore or get away from people who put you down or don't believe in your abilities.

- Professionally surround yourself, with people who have positive outlooks and similar goals to yours.

- Spend time with professionals (mentors and others) who are doing things that are similar to what you want to do. These should be people who believe in you and encourage your success.

Prepare

Preparation builds confidence,
courage, and competence.

O NE OF THE FIRST THINGS WOMEN IN GROWTH economies usually share with me is that lack of preparation has never been an option for them. A woman who wants a career or business in a growth economy simply won't succeed if she is *unprepared*.

Data from the International Labor Organization, a United Nations agency that tracks the global workforce, reveals two main reasons some women don't pursue work. They either are not prepared or don't have the resources or infrastructure they need to join the workforce.[1] Women thriving in their workplaces and succeeding in business have overcome these obstacles through consistent implementation of a powerful set of habits.

Competence: Keep Learning

T O PREPARE FOR SUCCESS, IT IS IMPORTANT TO BUILD A STRONG base of business knowledge and regularly hone your skills. Being highly competent is one way to overcome certain obstacles.

To continually expand and deepen your competence, get the job experience and build the skills that will help you the most. On-the-job, hands-on experience is usually the best way to learn. Training is the right learning option if you need to develop a new skill that you cannot readily acquire at work. Reading is most valuable when you want to broaden your base of knowledge. Feedback is most useful when you have the skill you need, but need to improve it.

If you work at a company that provides regular training opportunities, you are fortunate and should take full advantage of what is available. If you don't have such opportunities and you need to identify training opportunities in the marketplace, do some research before you sign up for a program. First, identify the competency you want to develop, and how you intend to use what you learn in your job or future jobs. Then evaluate programs for how effectively they meet your needs. Research the caliber and experience of the organization and the trainer providing the training. If you are able, get a recommendation from someone who has attended the program or other similar programs.

ACTIONS
TO DEVELOP COMPETENCE

Use the following three steps to develop a plan to increase your competencies.

1. Review your notes from the action section "Think with Confidence" (see page 27) to evaluate your areas of strength. Remember, the purpose of that exercise was to identify the skills you do well. Pick your two top strengths.

2. Pick two areas of knowledge or skill that you want to develop further. These can be areas of weakness or skills you think will be important to your career in the future.

3. Using the four methods of learning (learning from experience, feedback, reading, and attending training programs) build a learning plan for the four

skills you identified in Step 1 and Step 2 above. See the Sample Learning Plan below. On the next page, you'll find a blank table for you to complete your own learning plan.

SAMPLE LEARNING PLAN

SKILL	EXPERIENCE	FEEDBACK	READING	TRAINING/ CONFERENCE
Strength 1: Finance	Ask to take on additional financial responsibilities at work by X date			
Strength 2: Business Development	Implement two new sales techniques by year's end.	Go on three difficult or challenging customer calls with more experienced salespeople by X date.		Identify and attend a training program in advanced selling techniques.
New Area 1: Social Media			Do some online research on best ways to leverage social media every week.	
New Area 2: Mobile Tech		Ask questions about how people use mobile technology	Read about developments in the mobile space once a month.	

YOUR LEARNING PLAN

SKILL	EXPERIENCE	FEEDBACK

READING	TRAINING/CONFERENCE

Choose:
Define Your Success

DEFINE SUCCESS IN TERMS OF the long-term rewards you would like to experience both in your career and in other areas of your life. This is going to be very personal. You don't need to strive to meet anyone else's expectations, ideals, or goals. Keep yourself from measuring your success against another woman's desires and achievements. If you are true to yourself, then your life and happiness will be based on what you actually want.

Visualize your success!

Choosing your own success involves self-reflection and inquiry. Base your vision of success on what you feel passionate about and on your authentic desires. Give your vision time to reveal itself. Remember, success is a journey, so how you define it is likely to change as you follow your path and evolve.

Pay attention to what energizes you, not just what you are good at. Trust your passions and intuition in this process of self-discovery. There's no need to rush the process.

SELF-REFLECTION: IDENTIFY OPPORTUNITIES TO CONTRIBUTE

If you don't already know what success looks like for you, here are some questions to ponder and explore on your own or with loved ones in moments of quiet and peace. Think, dream, and talk about some or all of these questions. Pick the questions that resonate with you and make note of your responses.

- What is the real reason I am here?
  Examples: To make a difference in my community, for my family, or to be an example for my children.

- What do I stand for?
  Examples: Progress, change, truth, innovation, or women's rights.

- Who do I choose to be?
  Examples: An influential leader, a contributing member of my community, or a good mother.

- What evokes my intense interest and a desire to take action?
  Examples: The arts, fashion, technology, innovation, or legal matters.

- What is missing from my life right now?
  Examples: Independence or challenge.

- Why would I feel more complete with this missing piece?
  Examples: Because I would . . . feel a proud sense of accomplishment, know I had made a difference, have contributed to my family, feel more financially secure.

- What would I like to be doing that I am not doing?
  Examples: Working, running my own business, playing a senior role, or serving on a corporate or community board of directors.

- What would I feel really great about accomplishing?

- What would bring me joy, serenity, and fulfillment?

- What would bring me contentment?

The answers to these questions contain clues to help you define your success.

→ **ACTIONS**
   TO CHOOSE YOUR SUCCESS

Once you have your answers to the questions above and you are clearer about what is important and meaningful to you, the next step is to envision your successful life. Here's how. (If you need more room to respond, you can write more ideas in a journal.)

- Describe want you want your life to be like.
  Examples: I want to . . . have a career/business, make a lot of money (or be financially secure), be married, remain single, have children, not have children. I want my life to be busy or quiet, easy, challenging, and so on.

- Pinpoint the work you would enjoy that also enables you to have what you described in answers to the preceding questions.
  Examples: Holding a powerful leadership position in a large corporation, running my own business, working for a small company where I can have a lot of responsibility, or being part of a team and not have too much individual responsibility.

- Identify the businesses or ways in which you could realize your professional passions. If you don't know where these types of opportunities exist, share your insights with the professionally minded people you know and ask for their input.

  Examples: I could achieve what I want and believe I would enjoy working at . . . a bank, a startup company, a multinational company, an environmentally conscious small business, a family-owned business; or by being a consultant or starting my own independent business.

Summon the courage to choose what is most important and fulfilling to you. Find the strength and voice to explain your choices and develop the will to pursue what you want.

Create Your Plans

CREATING A CAREER OR business plan does not mean that you need to have your whole life mapped out. It means that you have a plan with targets and milestones that move you forward professionally. Begin with the desire to accomplish something specific. Start with your aspirations, even if they change once you begin to pursue them. From this intention, create a precise plan of short-term actions to take by a certain date and time. Plan out how you are going to accomplish each step. Find ways to stay on track, including reporting your progress to someone who will hold you accountable. Have confidence in your plan. Summon the courage to work your plan and to take the tough actions required to accomplish what you have set out to achieve.

Tangible goals you set and achieve will move you forward.

Some goals are more difficult to accomplish than others. Keep a plan B in your back pocket in case your plan A is thwarted. Understand that you won't be successful in attaining your goals 100 percent of the time. Regularly assess your plan. If your plan isn't bringing personal satisfaction, begin the process again by evaluating what is important to you and setting a new plan in motion.

As you define and redefine your personal definition of success, create a plan, set and reset goals, meet some goals, and miss others, you will continue to approach the vision of what's right for you.

SELF-REFLECTION:
YOUR GOALS

With your definition of success in mind, ask yourself these questions:

- Do I know what it will take to achieve what I want?
  Examples: Time, money, contacts, or other resources.

- Am I underestimating what I need to do and how hard it might be?

- Am I prepared to achieve the professional or business goals I want? If not, what knowledge or skills do I need?
  Examples: Financial skills, sales skills, or technical skills.

- What do I already know and have achieved that will give me the foundation to achieve success?
  Examples: A strong referral network. Prior similar types of achievements. Access to funds.

- What has already helped me get to where I am today?
  Examples: My expertise in X. My contacts with Y. My reputation.

- How much money and what type of support will it take for me to have the type of life I desire?

Working through these questions will help you define and narrow the goals you need to set to achieve your definition of success.

ACTIONS
TO ACHIEVE YOUR GOALS

Try using the following approach to set your goals. Imagine that you woke tomorrow morning and found that you had achieved your definition of success! See yourself in that place. Visualize and feel what it would be like. Are you with me? Great!

Now, from that perspective, go back and think about the steps you took to arrive at this great place. Group the steps together into overall actions. Use these as the basis for your goals, and then take the following steps to set and achieve your goals.

1. Set three or four goals (no more) that you can reach over several months—a year at the most. These are the short-term goals that will eventually get you to your long-term reward, the realization of the vision that is your personal definition of success.

    - Ensure that these goals are very clear and specific, and include the date by which you want to achieve them.
      Examples: By July 20XX, I will get three new clients worth X in revenue. By September, I will attend a training session to learn how to X.

    - Contrary to what you may have been taught in the past, set goals that you believe you can achieve—goals that are within your reach.

2. Set an intention to meet your goals. Then:
   - Write down your goals.
   - Put them someplace visible, where you can regularly see and focus on them.
     Example: Write them on big notes and put them on the wall above your desk.
   - Share your goals with someone you trust and to whom you feel accountable.

3. Plan how you will achieve your goals.
   - Break down each goal into specific steps you (or someone else) need to take.
   - Write down the first step you'll need to take for each goal and when and where (the date, time, and place) you'll take it.
   - Schedule specific times on your calendar to work on your goals.

4. Review your progress and results.

     ▪ Develop a system and schedule to review your progress. Spend time examining whether the actions you are taking are producing the outcomes you want, and whether or not you still want to achieve your original goals.

       Examples: Create a spreadsheet. Put the actions you intend to take in your calendar. Leave space beside them to track your impressions.

     ▪ Set up regular appointments with someone to whom you feel accountable in order to review the goals you set.

Remember, it is critical to develop a schedule that works for you. Identify your most productive and creative times of day. Know when you prefer dealing with people versus working alone. As you build a specific schedule of days and times of day to work on certain priorities, set up specific appointments in your schedule. Stick to those dates and times just like you would any other important appointment. Do not allow people or unimportant tasks to encroach on the time you have set aside to work on your goals.

Focus — get clear on what you want.

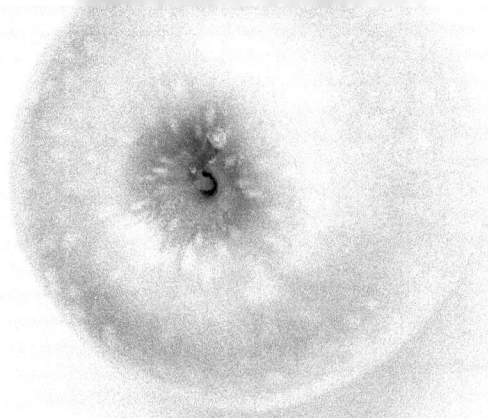

Customize:
Integrate Work into Life

T O DEVELOP YOUR INTEGRATED MINDSET, STOP VIEWING LIFE and work as either one or the other, combine them. Define what a successful integrated life looks like for you, and know that it will be different from most other women's lifestyles. Look at your life and your priorities. Use the focus habit to define your success. Then determine how the people around you can help you create the life you desire, and leverage the resources you need. Finally, make specific and careful schedules so that your work and life fit well together.

Choosing to build an integrated life may require adjusting many things at home and at work, but it will be one of the best decisions you can make for your happiness and personal definition of success.

Instead of thinking about if you can "have it all," think about designing your life so you may have what matters to you. Consider your own personal and family needs, as well as your values, career aspirations, and goals. Think also about the support you need and want to receive, especially the emotional support and the money that's required to have the life you envision. Given everything involved in creating an integrated life, how could your wants and needs look like anyone else's? Your life goals are individual to you.

SELF-REFLECTION:
WHAT DOES YOUR CUSTOMIZED LIFE LOOK LIKE?

Start by envisioning what your integrated life looks like and how you'd like each piece of your life (you, your family, work, friends, and other interests) to fit together. If you cannot envision how they integrate, it will be impossible for anyone else (your husband, boss, family, and so on) to do so. Seek your own "right" combination between the amount of time needed for work and at home, between work and family needs, between work and play, and between your own needs and desires and those of others. Your vision should answer the following questions.

- What do you want your integrated life to look like?

  Examples: Think about commitments you want to make to family or community, about hours or times you want to commit to work, about a person whose integrated life you respect. How do they do it? Think about what you want realistic days to look like in your integrated life.

- Next, ask:
  - How much do I want to work?

  - How hard am I willing to work?

- How much time do I want outside of work?

- How do I want to spend my time outside work?

- What level of stress am I willing to have at work and in the rest of my life?

- How much responsibility do I want to have at work?

- How much responsibility do I want to have at home?

• What measures will you use to know when and if you have achieved an integrated life?

Examples: You are able to get home from work to participate in some of your children's activities. You have time to be alone with your husband. You schedule for yourself and the activities you care about. You are spending sufficient time focused on your job or business to produce stellar results.

These indicators should be directly linked to your definition of success.

→ ACTIONS
TO CUSTOMIZE YOUR LIFE

Challenging problems are often best solved by taking a series of repeated actions. You could choose to view the challenge of fitting work into life as intractable; after all, it is arguably an age-old problem, one that some would say has dogged every woman who ever worked outside her home. Or you could do what millions of women around the world do every day, and make work-life integration a habit comprised of many small steps. Stitched together, these create the rich fabric of your life.

Think about your integrated life in four main quadrants:

Self	Family
Work	Community

An integrated life is not a matter of spending equal amounts of time in each quadrant, or of one quadrant taking precedence over another. Instead, it's about paying attention to the parts of each of the quadrants that matter most to you. At various times in your life you'll make decisions about how much time you want or need to spend in each quadrant. Be open to changing how much time you spend in each area as you progress in your goals.

Here are some steps you can take.

1. Map out a schedule that accommodates your life and work priorities.

2. Have a conversation at home about what you want professionally. Share with your family why you want to work, why it's important to you to work, and your ideas about schedule support, and so on. Be sure you outline the roles you'd like your family members to take on. Frame the conversation as an open discussion, not as a demand, and be open to ideas, alternatives, and suggestions made by your loved ones.

3. Have a conversation at work about your professional goals in the context of your life's priorities. Schedule a specific time to meet with your manager and your team (if appropriate). Begin by clearly stating how important work is to you and your commitment to the company and your career. Explain that in order to do the best possible job at work, you also need to be able to manage your other life priorities. Simply and directly ask for what you need. If you are asking for flexibility or work schedule changes, be sure you have think through how your work will be handled. Your message will be best received if you thought through the details ahead of time. Remember, no apologies. Give your manager time to consider your needs and get back to you with his/her agreement or alternatives.

4. Don't ask for help. Instead, ask people to do the part they need to do.

When women ask their husbands, children, or colleagues and staff at work to help them do something, they retain the idea that the task is their responsibility and the other person is merely "helping" them temporarily. If instead, we politely ask the person to do the task, then it becomes their own. For example, instead of saying, "Would you please help me fold the laundry?" say, "The laundry needs to be folded. Please fold it." Instead of saying, "Would you please help me by running this report or creating this presentation?" say, "The client needs this report, please run it."

5. Don't apologize about work at home, and don't apologize about personal or home needs at work.

In your personal life with your family, your partner, and especially with your children and friends, don't apologize for needing to work. Instead be excited and proud about your professional activities.

- When you are at work, don't apologize about your personal life; be excited about your family and leisure-time interests.

- Learn to be comfortable with your right to make personal and professional decisions that work best for you.

- When you are excited about the things you are doing, others will be excited along with you and will understand why you are at the other place, or why you do what brings you fulfillment.

- If you talk about work as drudgery and you constantly apologize, those around you will see this and perhaps attempt to make you feel guilty. If you apologize for your needs and the needs of your family, then your coworkers won't be conditioned to understand and respect your priorities.

Many of us are conditioned to apologize for anything that affects other people. Stopping this habit can feel foreign, uncomfortable, or even dangerous to our relationships. However, the people around you will start to see that you have not changed your personality or sold out your culture, but that you have simply become more secure in how you operate at work and in your life. Maintain the respectful and courteous habits central to your culture and the need to apologize will fade away.

Although on the surface not apologizing may seem like a minor tactic, it's actually much more significant than that because it has to do with your mindset and how you communicate. It is a very tangible action that you can use to begin to change the conversation about your priorities. You will also begin to see a shift in how your family, those around you, and your employer think about you regarding your work and personal life. Best of all, not being apologetic really works!

COMMUNICATE WITHOUT APOLOGIZING

DON'T SAY . . .	INSTEAD SAY . . .
At home: "I am so sorry I won't be able to be home for dinner tonight. I have a meeting."	"I have an important meeting tonight that will (explain its relevance or how it helps you with your work). It will be great to catch up and hear about your day when I get home."
At home: "I am so sorry, Mommy can't take you to/pick you up from school tomorrow."	Guess what I get to do tomorrow? I am going to X. What fun things are you going to get to do at school tomorrow? You'll be going to school with Y. It will be fun to catch up on what happened during our day when we see each other later."
At work: "I am so sorry, but I have to leave to pick up my kid (or go to the doctor, go out with my husband, and so on)."	"I've got to head out now to X. I'll work on this tomorrow/later tonight. We'll get it done."

Contribute: Be Notable, Make an Impact

Meet mentor at 2pm

T O ACCELERATE YOUR SUCCESS, KEEP GROWING AND LEARNING. Acquire and continue to develop the interpersonal, managerial, leadership, and technical skills required to excel in your field.

You will need to seek new skill-development opportunities even if you are content in your current position or business. Otherwise you will start to decline, sometimes even unconsciously. Professionally speaking, staying still results in decline. No one ever overcame a barrier or obstacle by standing still.

You have to fly above, not below the radar. By that, I mean that you and your results must be visible and notable. The ways to become notable are to:

- Achieve tangible business results.
- Communicate your achievements.
- Convey a strong professional presence.

To accelerate your career success, contribute results, make your achievements known, and cultivate a strong professional presence.

(?)   ## SELF-REFLECTION:
IDENTIFY OPPORTUNITIES TO CONTRIBUTE

Answer the following three questions to determine where you can best contribute.

- How does my company or business succeed in the marketplace? What financial, strategic, and customer measures are most important for its success? Examples: Through customer acquisition, large contracts, or new product launches.

- Where and how do I fit into the essential, most valued parts of the business? Which of my skills and competencies could make the best contribution? Examples: Social media, contract negotiation, financial analysis, or strategic product innovation.

- Which of these competencies do I most enjoy? And which comes most easily to me?

Here are some of the specific actions I share when I coach my clients to accelerate their success.

→ ACTIONS
TO CONTRIBUTE RESULTS

Once you have determined the metrics and levers that drive performance where you work, find ways to deliver results in those areas. The best way to do that is to:

- Identify one or two areas of opportunity for your company or industry that intersect with your interests, strengths, and areas of expertise.

- Determine a specific outcome you can achieve in this area/these areas.

- Make time in your schedule to work on the area or areas you identify.

→ ACTIONS
TO COMMUNICATE YOUR CONTRIBUTIONS

Take the following steps to communicate your contributions.

1. For every one of your significant accomplishments, identify specifically whom you should share the achievement with.
   Examples: My manager, an influential leader, or my mentor.

2. Determine the most strategic timing for you to communicate. Assess when your communication will be best received and won't get buried under a mountain of other information.

3. Determine how you will make your accomplishment known to your manager and influential others.
   Examples: Send a note or email. Verbally share your achievement. Find someone who is willing to share news of your achievement on your behalf. Take out an advertisement in a trade publication. Write an article.

4. Share the outcomes you produce, not just activities you are engaged in. Describe your contributions in a manner consistent with the way that people in your industry, community, or company measure results. Use business language and measures of performance that are understood and valued in your field.

5. For really notable achievements, consider applying for, or being nominated for an award or competition.

There are numerous recognition initiatives for businesswomen all over the world. There may even be some at your place of employment. Do some research online to identify programs and ask your mentors, network, or businesswomen's organization about such programs they may know of. These recognition programs are an excellent way for you to indirectly communicate news of your achievements and become better known in the business community.

Select one or more of these approaches, or identify another way that feels comfortable and is appropriate in your culture. You don't have to brag, and your communication style can be humble, but you must find a way to make your successes known.

ACTIONS
TO ACKNOWLEDGE YOUR CONTRIBUTIONS

My mother always told me that when someone pays you a compliment, it is exactly the same as if they had given you a gift. The appropriate response when someone gives you a gift is to say, "Thank you." So why, when most of us have been taught to be kind and gracious, can we not accept compliments or positive feedback?

Every time your performance or results are recognized, thank the person recognizing you, then accept and take credit for the result rather than dismissing, diminishing, or minimizing your performance. Because acknowledging and communicating your contributions is so important to raising your visibility and accelerating your success, following are some specific ways you can do so.

INSTEAD OF SAYING THINGS LIKE . . .	SAY . . .
When someone acknowledges one of your accomplishments: • "We have been given many opportunities." • "I have a great team." • "We've been lucky."	• "Thank you. I have I am proud/ pleased with my role (leading or as a member of our team) and the results achieved." • "Thank you. I worked hard (along with the team) to make this successful." • "Thank you. I am glad that you see my hard work (and my team's work) reflected in our results."
When someone compliments one of your ideas: "It was nothing, everyone has good ideas."	"Thank you. I'm glad my input was helpful and can add value to our work."
When someone presents you with an opportunity: "I hope I can meet your expectations."	"Thank you. I look forward to making a significant contribution."

ACTIONS
TO BUILD YOUR PROFESSIONAL PRESENCE

Your professional presence also sends messages about your goals to those around you. As you think about strengthening your presence, take the following actions.

• Speak like a businessperson.

Examples: Communicate in a direct, crisp, and succinct way. Have an expert grasp of the business terminology and vocabulary of your field. Use this language as your means to contribute your best business insights or ideas.

• Maintain an appearance that's in line with company-wide, industry, and cultural norms even as it expresses your personal style. Avoid dishevelment.

- Behave in a manner that is consistent with cultural and corporate norms.

- Be poised.
  Examples: Project confidence. Demonstrate calm and control.
  Emulate the most successful people around you. Communicate clearly
  and maintain your composure.

To maintain composure under any circumstances, pay attention to the overall impression you make. Everything matters, including how you stand, sit, look, talk, and react.

If conforming to cultural or business expectations creates too much tension for you and requires you not to be true to yourself, then adapting is not right for you. Just be aware that the world probably won't mold itself to your preferences. If you want to develop your professional presence, try these specific communication techniques.

IF YOU HAVE A TENDENCY TO . . .	INSTEAD . . .
Talk too much	• **Start in the middle.** When you want to communicate something, don't start at the beginning of the story or incident, start from the middle. Remember, people will ask if they need more background information. • **Pick**. If you have five things you want to say, pick the most important three. If you have three things you want to say, pick two.

66

Achieve results and make notable contributions.

	• **Visualize a traffic sign**. When you start talking, visualize that the light is green for one minute. After one minute, the light turns orange. At that point you have thirty seconds to find a clear indication that your audience is engaged and actively listening to you. If they are, you may talk for another minute before the light turns red. If not, slow down at orange and ask if they want you to continue or have any questions.
Speak too little	• **Look for a pause** in conversation when others are talking, and insert your perspective. • **Tell a trusted coworker or your manager** that you are working on communicating more frequently. Ask your ally to bring you into more conversations by asking you questions or referencing your areas of expertise.
Speak primarily in tactical terms	• **Prepare** a strategic point of view before every meeting or important conversation. • **Group** your comments under strategic statements or categories.
Speak too casually and not use business terms	• **Listen** to those around you who use business terminology well. Notice which business terms and metrics they use, and follow their example. • **Learn** how your company makes money and what it values by speaking with your manager, a financial person, or by reading. Incorporate financial metrics and things that are important to your company, business, or industry when you talk about your own work.
Get flustered	• **Anticipate** negative triggers and prepare in advance how you will deal with them. • **Take a deep breath** and silently, slowly count to ten before you speak. • **Stand firmly.** Sometimes something as seemingly small as how you stand can affect the way you respond. Observe your standing or sitting posture, and adjust it accordingly so that you feel firmly anchored when you deliver your message.

Connect:
Nurture Your Network

Meet mentor
at 2pm

BUILDING YOUR PROFESSIONAL NETWORK AND HAVING MENTORS and sponsors helps you get the opportunities that lead to success as you have defined it. Use what you know, your contacts, and the contributions you make to seek out opportunities. There are ample opportunities available for women with education, skills, confidence, and drive.

To supercharge your success, your career or business advancement plan should include:

- A strong network with four types of connections: up (more senior people), down (more junior people), in (your organization), and out (people in your field and community).
- Mentoring.
- Gaining opportunities through your own initiative and perhaps through the support of a sponsor.

Use the following self-reflection activities and action steps to improve your network.

(?) SELF-REFLECTION:
WHAT'S THE QUALITY OF YOUR NETWORK?

Assess your network in the following ways.

- Do I have a deep and broad network, a limited network, or a small-to-nonexistent network? Use the Up, Down, In, and Out framework to evaluate how many people and the type of people you are connected with.

- How frequently and in what manner do I connect with the people in my network?

- What are my preferred and most comfortable ways to network?
  Examples: At events, one on one, online.

⊙→ ## ACTIONS
     ## TO STRENGTHEN YOUR NETWORK

Take the following actions to broaden and deepen your network.

- Based on your career or business goals, identify three to five people you'd like to connect with or with whom you'd like to renew contact.

- Based on your preferred style of networking, identify where your best chances of connecting with your targets are—and how to do so.
  Examples: Through a mutual contact or a mutual organization, at an upcoming event, or via an email introduction.

- Make a plan with a specific time to reach out and connect with the people you have identified.

SELF-REFLECTION:
WHAT KIND OF MENTORING ARE YOU GIVING
AND GETTING?

Evaluate your mentoring. A mentor is someone who gives sound and relevant advice, often based on his or her experience.

- Am I getting the type of mentoring and advice I need to help me achieve success as I define it?

- How often do my mentors and I meet?

- Am I mentoring anyone?

- How often do I meet with the people I'm mentoring?

→ ACTIONS
TO ELEVATE YOUR GUIDANCE

Remember that maintaining and strengthening your network takes attention and effort. You may need to make changes to your schedule or priorities in order to get the type of mentoring you want.

- If you are getting the type of mentoring you need, express your gratitude to your mentors and share with them how their guidance is helping you.

- If you feel that you need additional guidance, identify someone from your network who you believe would be helpful to you.

- If you are already a mentor, commend yourself for the guidance you are providing.

- If you are not yet a mentor, identify someone you can help, and begin a relationship with them.

ⓘ SELF-REFLECTION:
ARE YOU READY FOR A SPONSOR?

If you are ready to take your career or business to the next level you would likely benefit from having a sponsor. A sponsor is someone who has the seniority, stature, and power to advocate for you. They use their influence to create more business or career opportunities for you.

Evaluate whether you are ready for a sponsor by asking the following questions.

- Am I a strong performer who consistently works on her professional development, and who shows initiative in taking on new work assignments?

- Do I make significant contributions and create results for my organization?

- Am I known by this potential sponsor and well thought of by him or her? Ways to become known include volunteering to work on projects, committees, initiatives, and/or community activities that the potential sponsor is leading and is passionate about.

66

Surround yourself with supportive likeminded people, familiar with your strengths and contributions.

- Do I know how I'd like my career to develop and what sorts of future roles I'd like to take? Can I articulate my desires to my potential sponsor?

If you answered yes to the questions above, take the following actions to connect with a potential sponsor.

ACTIONS
TO HELP YOU CONNECT WITH A POTENTIAL SPONSOR

If you can answer yes to all of the above questions, then on your own or through a mentor, begin to build a relationship with a senior leader at your organization or in your industry at large who has the power and influence to serve as your sponsor. If you cannot answer yes to all five questions, continue to improve your skills and results. Slowly and carefully cultivate a relationship with people in your network as outlined earlier.

— HABIT 6: LEAD —

Change: Forge a New Path

YOU BECOME A LEADER AS SOON AS YOU DECIDE WHEN, WHERE, and how you want to lead. There will be times when you will see that you are the one who can solve a problem or create change that makes a difference. As you assume personal responsibility to make things better, you'll be leading.

As with other success habits, the habit of leading starts inside—with your own thoughts and beliefs—and requires bold action. Your leadership doesn't have to resemble a stereotyped image. Lead in your own way. Start by identifying opportunities for improvement and change. Lead by gathering information, thinking strategically about the future, proactively sharing your ideas and solutions. Lead from where you are and lead by your example.

Whether you would like to lead by developing new products and services, by improving existing systems, by heading a business or community initiative, or by committing yourself to one-on-one relationships, you can identify excellent opportunities to lead by observing, listening, and gathering information. Then be undeterred in sharing your vision or example for change.

SELF-REFLECTION:
WHAT CAN YOU CHANGE?

To identify your opportunities to lead, ask yourself:

- What do I care most about?

- What can I influence or change?

- Is there a situation or issue that I can improve?

- What has not been thought of that should be considered?

- What has not been done that should be done?

66

You will make the greatest impact when you create new paths and new ways of doing things for yourself and others.

- What changes do I or others think are needed?

- Where are there unmet needs?

- What could be done better?

- What are the direction and strategy of the company where I work?

- What is important to my company's success?

- What is the biggest influence on my company's profitability?

- What do the CEO and executive management team care most about?

- What do the customers care most about?

⊙→ ## ACTIONS
TO BRING ABOUT CHANGE

Take what you uncovered in your self-reflection and then:

- **Start where you are.**
  Think about what you know and what you are good at. Start from the role you are in. No matter what position you occupy, you *can* lead. You have the knowledge, information, and insights to make a difference.

- **Make connections from what you uncover.**
  This is where women have an advantage. We are good listeners, observers, and learners. Take the information you've been gathering and envision a new way or a better way.
  Examples: Identify problems, pain points, and opportunities. Bring ideas from one industry into another to provide fresh, new improvements. Bring experiences from situations that are similar to the situation you want to improve.

- **Speak up and propose ideas.**
  Examples: Be bold and specific in your proposal. Present your ideas in business language and explain how results can be measured. Use a combination of written material, images, and conversation to convey your leadership ability. Apply what you have seen other effective leaders do in similar situations.

- **Be an example of how you think something should be done.**
  If people are resistant to change or unwilling to do things in a new way, demonstrate leadership by doing what needs to be done in the new or better way.

- **Anticipate challenges and failures.**
  If you can anticipate what your challenges will be and who might challenge you, you can talk to people in advance, work to build support, and then make some adjustments in your approach that make it easier for your ideas to be heard and accepted. Making mistakes is okay if they help you do better the next time.

You have come full circle from where we started at the beginning of this workbook. To clear obstacles, you have to be undeterred by the things that come between you and what you want to achieve. But to completely remove obstacles so they are no longer there for you or anyone else requires something more. It requires leadership to change systems and challenge the status quo. To find lasting solutions, you have to be innovative and resourceful. **You have to lead!**

66

You are in a time and place where success is possible for you!

A FINAL WORD

CONGRATULATIONS! BY WORKING THROUGH THE *I AM UNDETERRED* exercises, you have created your success plan for the immediate future, which can change your life if you execute it. Always remember to pair reflection with action. Once you're clear, you'll find that the actions follow much more easily than you may have originally imagined they would.

More and more women around the world are changing their lives by starting businesses and jumping into careers that stimulate their hearts and minds every day. I am excited for you because you are now part of a global movement. None of us has wait to wait for someone else to make change for us so we can be successful. Success and change begins the day we decide to do it for ourselves.

I would love to hear from you about your success plan and the undeterred progress you are making. Let me extend my sincere invitation to you right now to join the broader community of undeterred women worldwide and engage in a dialogue with us by visiting The Way Women Work.com. Also feel free to send me an email at raniaanderson@thewaywomenwork.com.

66

All that remains now is that you stay undeterred.

Or reach out to me via social media with the hashtag #IAMUNDETERRED. If you like, take a photo of yourself with *Undeterred* or this workbook, and post it on your social networks. Use the hashtag #IAMUNDETERRED. When you do this, you will be joining a conversation with countless other aspiring professional women all over the world who are reading this book. You will also inspire other women to be undeterred and to work on their own success plans.

I have no doubt that whatever you set your mind to you can accomplish!

IF YOU'D LIKE MORE

CONNECT WITH THE WAY WOMEN WORK

Thank you for reading *Undeterred*. I hope you feel more prepared, focused, and determined to accelerate your success. Visit TheWayWomenWork.com, where you'll find:

- Stories of businesswomen in growth economies.
- Tips, tools, and strategies.
- Career guidance from me.
- A complimentary monthly newsletter.
- Our blog. Note that we accept guest post submissions. Let us know if you'd like share the story of your work experience to help other women in growth economies.

ORDER *UNDETERRED* AND ADDITIONAL COPIES OF THIS WORKBOOK

I Am Undeterred is a companion for readers of *Undeterred*. It includes the complete set of self-reflection and action exercises to help you practice the six success habits of women in emerging economies. To order copies of *Undeterred* go to TheWayWomenWork. com/undeterred. Bulk order discounts are available to universities, schools, organizations, and other institutions.

HIRE ME TO SPEAK FOR YOUR COMPANY OR EVENT

If you'd like to have me come speak, you can reach me at http://raniaanderson.com.

SOCIAL MEDIA

I invite you to connect with me on social networks.

- *Twitter:* http://twitter.com/thewaywomenwork
- *Facebook:* https://www.facebook.com/TheWayWomenWork
- *Pinterest:* http://www.pinterest.com/thewaywomenwork

I'd love to hear from you. Share your thoughts about what has inspired you in your career or business, and what you've learned from reading the book. Don't be shy! Go ahead and show me, take a photo of yourself with *Undeterred* or *I Am Undeterred*, and post it on your social networks. Use the hashtag #IAMUNDETERRED.

ABOUT THE AUTHOR

Rania Habiby Anderson IS A LEADING EXPERT ON THE professional advancement of businesswomen in developing and emerging economies and an executive coach.

Originally from the Middle East, Rania has lived and traveled all over the developing world. Her early career success was at Bank of America, where she progressed to a senior leadership role. She left the bank in 1997 to start an executive coaching and consulting business. For the past seventeen years, Rania has coached businesswomen and businessmen around the world.

Fueled by a deep belief that women are the key to global economic prosperity and a lifelong desire to eradicate gender inequality and help women thrive, in 2010, Rania founded The Way Women Work, an online career advice platform visited daily by hundreds of women from around the world.

Rania is a global speaker, cofounder of a women's angel investor network, a devoted mentor, and a contributor to business publications. She holds a master's degree in foreign service with an honors concentration in international business from Georgetown University and a bachelor's degree with a major in business from Oklahoma State University.

www.ingramcontent.com/pod-product-compliance
Lightning Source LLC
Chambersburg PA
CBHW080939030426
42339CB00009B/477

* 9 7 8 0 9 9 0 9 0 6 3 3 9 *